MISSIONS
AND YOU!

Be a part of what God is doing in today's world

Larry W. Caldwell

OMF LITERATURE INC.

Manila, Philippines

MISSIONS AND YOU!
Be a Part of what God is Doing in Today's World
Copyright © 1994, 2009, 2019 by Larry W. Caldwell

Originally published in the Philippines under the title
Missions and You!
Copyright © 1994 by Larry W. Caldwell
Published by OMF Literature Inc.

Cover design by Nixon L. Na
Page design by Marianne C. Ventura

Published (2019) in the Philippines by
OMF Literature Inc.
776 Boni Avenue
Mandaluyong City, Metro Manila
www.OMFLit.com

Reprinted — 1995, 2000 (new cover), 2009 (revised and new format), 2011, 2013, 2019 (revised and updated)

ISBN 978-971-009-870-5

Printed in the Philippines

CONTENTS

To Mary
My partner in missions for over 40 years

PREFACE

THIS REVISED THIRD EDITION comes twenty-five years after the first publication of this little book. I am humbled to see how these pages have been used in the lives of so many missionaries over the years, missionaries who are currently on the front lines ministering to unreached people groups. The message of this book is simple, but I believe its implications are profound for us all.

We have seen many changes in the world of missions over the last twenty-five years. I highlight just four. The first change is the significant increase in the number of non-Western missionaries who are engaged in unreached peoples ministries. This is exciting! This is not to say that Western missionaries are no longer needed. Every Christian group and each believer shares equally the responsibility to carry out the Great Commission, regardless of nationality or country of birth. But it is to say that Western missionaries may have different roles to play in reaching unreached peoples today, now that so many non-Western missionaries are also taking up this task.

A second change is the increasing numbers of "scattered" or "diaspora" people groups. While people groups have been on the move throughout history, we are seeing the unprecedented movement of people groups today. As I write this there are almost 200 million individuals on the move today, individuals who are no longer living in the country that they were born in. Many of them have left their home countries voluntarily. Others have left involuntarily because of war, persecution or famine. These diaspora peoples are literally scattered all over the globe. Many of them are also unreached peoples (you will read about unreached peoples later in this book). What all this means is that missions is no longer somewhere "over there." Missions now may be to your diaspora neighbor living next door, or working in your office building, or attending your school. What an opportunity for churches today!

A third change is the increasing acceptance even among Evangelicals of inclusivism. In a nutshell, inclusivism is the idea that there are many ways to get to heaven and that Christianity is but one way. From a human perspective, it would be nice to believe that inclusivism were true. Who wouldn't want lots of good Muslims, Hindus and Buddhists in heaven along with Christians? But the reality is that such inclusivistic thinking eliminates the need for the Gospel and for Christian witness. Such inclusivistic thinking eliminates the need for missionaries. The Bible, however, makes very clear that there is only one way to heaven and that is through Jesus alone. If we lose this biblical truth we have lost the very essence of the Gospel.

A fourth change over the last twenty-five years is the number of unreached peoples in the world today. When this book was first published there were some 2.3 billion unreached peoples. Fifteen years later the number was 2.8 billion. Today the number is 3.3 billion. Most of this growth is due to increases in population because of the birth of more babies. Unfortunately, over this same twenty-five year period, the number of missionaries ministering to the unreached peoples has stayed essentially the same: around five percent of all missionaries deployed worldwide. These sobering facts remind us that, no matter what anybody might say, the day of the missionary is not over. Missions is not dead. We desperately need more missionaries if we truly mean to obey the Great Commission.

Thus the continuing need for this little book, *Missions and You!* God bless you as you consider what God has in mind for you in regard to missions.

chapter one

WHY
SHOULD YOU
GET INVOLVED?

"Therefore go and make disciples of all nations . . ."
MATTHEW 28:19–20

YES, WHY GET INVOLVED?

Isn't the job finished?

Churches seem to be everywhere. At least this is true in many countries in the world today. But does this mean that Jesus' command, given in His Great Commission, to "Go and make disciples of all nations," (Matthew 28:19–20) has been fulfilled? Is the job really finished? Can Christians now relax and take it easy until Jesus returns?

No! If you think it's time to relax then I have some bad news for you. The job isn't over yet. The command of Jesus, to "Go and make disciples of all nations," is relevant still for all Christians living in today's world.

Examine the facts

Let's look at some facts. Today in our world there are almost eight billion people.[1] That's an eight with nine zeros after it, as in

$$8,000,000,000!$$

Just how many of these eight billion people are Christians? If the job were almost done then we would

---

[1] Current world population projections estimate that by the year 2023 there will be eight billion people living on the earth.

expect that most of the eight billion would already be Christians. Unfortunately, that just isn't so. Look carefully at the following pieces of the POPULATION PIE:[2]

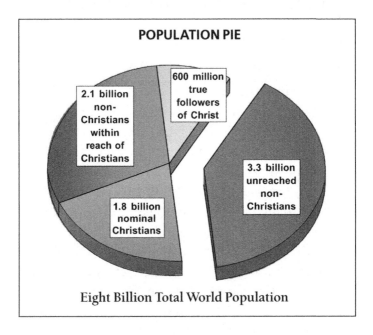

POPULATION PIE

600 million true followers of Christ

2.1 billion non-Christians within reach of Christians

3.3 billion unreached non-Christians

1.8 billion nominal Christians

Eight Billion Total World Population

So what should we make of the POPULATION PIE? Notice, first of all, which is the smallest piece of the pie. That's right, it's the number of true, born-again, Bible-believing Christ-followers, some 800 million in all. (I'm sorry if you were hoping for a bigger piece!)

Now look at the other pieces of the pie. There are

---

[2] Most of the statistics and the specific people group information presented in this chapter have been taken from the Joshua Project. Their website is found at www.joshuaproject.net. The numbers found in this Population Pie are based on the 2019 statistics of the Joshua Project extrapolated for a total population figure of eight billion.

some 1.8 billion nominal Christians — Christians in need of renewal. These are Christians who go to church and who call themselves Christians but who are not really on fire for the Lord.

Another piece of the pie comprises the approximately 2.1 billion individuals who are not yet Christians but *who have the opportunity to hear the Good News of Jesus if other local Christians will just tell them*. Many of them in fact have already heard the Gospel several times, but have chosen to reject it.

The last group — by far the largest piece of the pie — is made up of those individuals who have never heard the Gospel and will never hear it unless some Christian goes and tells them. It's not that this group has chosen to reject the Gospel, rather they have never heard a credible presentation of it in the first place. Most have had no exposure to the Gospel. There are some 3.3 billion of these individuals. Did you catch that? There are

3,300,000,000 people

living in the world today who will never hear about Jesus unless some Christian like you or me goes to tell them. Some of the pieces of the pie are probably a lot bigger than you thought they were. This is truly some food for thought.

It's really true
Hopefully the POPULATION PIE doesn't give you indigestion, unless it's of the spiritual kind. Yes, indeed,

the hearts of all Christians ought to skip a beat when faced with the stark reality: nearly three billion people in the world today either have never ever heard of Jesus Christ, or they haven't heard enough about Him to make a responsible decision for or against Him.

"Come on," some of you are saying. "Are there really people in today's world who have never heard?" I asked the same question myself many years ago before my wife and I went to teach at a university in the People's Republic of China. This was in 1983, a time when China was just opening up to the West. We had intelligent, well-educated Chinese students in our classes. In spite of their credentials most of these students had never before heard mention of God, or of Jesus, or even of the Bible. In fact, some of our students knew more about Santa Claus than about Jesus Christ! So I no longer ask if there are really people in the world who haven't heard. I know without a doubt that there are over three billion individuals just like those Chinese students.

Three billion seems like a huge number, and it is. But the good news is that reaching these three billion with the Gospel isn't the impossible task it may first appear to be. Why is that? Because each of these three billion individuals can be *found* in one of about 7,000 *people groups*. Seven thousand is a much easier number to deal with than three billion, right? But just what is a people group?

People groups
A people group is made up of individuals distinguished from others because they share a common language

and culture, and typically a common social and economic status.

In other words, if individuals all speak the same mother language and are a part of the same culture, then they probably are of the same people group. Most people groups can be determined by language and culture. However, people who speak the same mother language may need to be reached by significantly different strategies even if they are from the same people group.

For example, Filipino (which is largely based on the Tagalog language) is the mother tongue of many who live in the city of Manila, Philippines. But not all Filipino speakers are alike. There is a vast economic gulf between the minority of native Filipino speakers of the middle and upper classes of Manila and the hundreds of thousands of Filipino-speaking people who also live in Manila but in lower class homes, urban poor and slum communities. The economic disparities allow us to recognise distinct sub-groups among Filipino speakers in spite of their shared language. Different mission strategies may be appropriate to reach some of these sub-groups effectively.

Throughout the world there are estimated to be some 17,000 distinct people groups. Almost 10,000 of these people groups have already been reached with the Gospel of Christ, or can at least be considered "reachable." That leaves some 7,000 groups who are still unreached.

Unreached people groups
So what makes a particular people group an unreached people group? Here's a technical definition:

> An unreached people group is a people group among which there is no indigenous community of believing Christians with adequate numbers and resources to evangelize their own people without outside (cross-cultural) assistance.

Let's examine this definition. It describes two situations. First, if a people group has no Christians, or just a handful, then that group is clearly an unreached people group. Second, if there are Christians within the people group, and even churches, but not enough Christians and churches to effectively evangelize the people without outside help, then that group is an unreached people group. Unreached people groups range in size. Some may have a population of millions (like the four million Hazara found in Afghanistan, Iran, and Pakistan, or the sixteen million Khmer living in Cambodia and Vietnam), while others may be numbered merely in thousands (like the 6,000 Aralle of Indonesia or the 9,000 Sharwa living in Cameroon).

Let's look at an example
In the nation of Turkey there is a people group known as the Zaza-Dimli, numbering almost two million. This Muslim Kurdish people group inhabits the middle-eastern part of Turkey. Most of them are nomadic

people, moving around as they shepherd their livestock. Because of the ruggedness of their location they are not accessible by road. Zaza-Dimli Kurds living here are also isolated religiously, because they are passionate followers of the "Alevi Sect" of Islam, a mystical faith with strong shamanistic and Zoroastrian roots. As a result, other Muslims in Turkey, who follow the Sunni way, view the Zaza-Dimli as heretics. The Turkish government, likewise, is antagonistic towards them.

What all this comes down to is this: there are only a handful of Zaza-Dimli believers, not nearly enough to evangelize the rest of their own people group. The two million Zaza-Dimli, therefore, constitute an unreached people group. Reaching these Zaza-Dimli will require outside cross-cultural assistance until the Zaza-Dimli believers have enough members and churches to evangelize their own people on their own.

Remember this:

> An *unreached people group* will become a *reached people group* only when Christians from *another reached people group* go and take the Good News of Jesus to them.

These 7,000 unreached people groups of the world can be divided into five major categories:

Muslim (with some 3,000 groups),
Hindu (2,500 groups),
Buddhist (500 groups),

Chinese (300 groups), and
Other (700 groups).

Another way of looking at these five major categories is found in the UNREACHED PEOPLES PIE below.

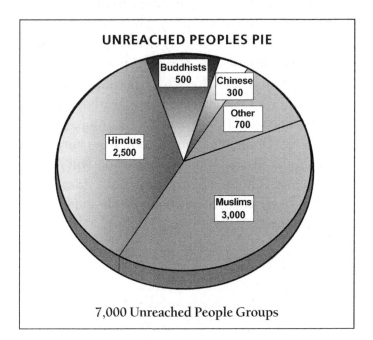

UNREACHED PEOPLES PIE

Buddhists 500

Chinese 300

Other 700

Hindus 2,500

Muslims 3,000

7,000 Unreached People Groups

Missions experts and missions organizations have already gathered much specific information on the majority of these unreached people groups.[3] What is needed now is enough Christians committed to reaching them.

---

[3] See Chapter Six for a listing of some of the better websites dealing with unreached people groups.

Unreached people groups and the 10/40 window

OK, so there are some 7,000 unreached people groups in the world today. "But just where are they?" you ask. Good question. Actually, pockets of unreached peoples are found in virtually every major city of the world. For example, international students from many of these unreached people groups can be found on most university campuses in the United States and also among the students in universities in many other countries. It is oftentimes a lot easier to bring the Gospel to them on the university campus than in their home countries. There are hundreds of Muslim Pakistani nurses working in countries in the Middle East. They are much more open to other expatriate Christian nurses sharing Jesus with them in those countries than they would be — or could be — in Pakistan. In Manila there are thousands of Hindus from India. In the Los Angeles school system over a hundred different languages are spoken, each representing people groups of at least 10,000 individuals. Conclusion:

> You don't necessarily have to go overseas to reach some of these unreached people groups. *They may already be living right in your neighborhood!*

The whole concept of reaching an unreached people group seems more manageable once we realize that most of the 7,000 unreached people groups in the world are found in one major geographical area known as the "10/40 Window."

The 10/40 Window defines an area found between 10° (ten degrees) north and 40° (forty degrees) north of the equator, hence the designation "10/40." This area extends from Western Africa across the Middle East and Asia. Almost sixty of the world's least-evangelized countries fall within or near the boundaries of the 10/40 Window. Most of the world's unreached peoples, including the majority of all Muslims, Hindus and Buddhists, live within this region. The following map shows the geographical area of this "Window."

THE 10/40 WINDOW

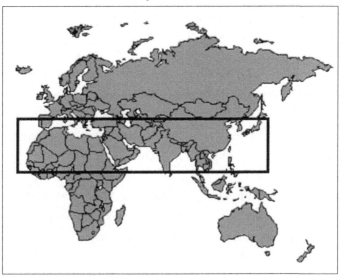

Not only do we now know who most of the unreached people groups are, we also know where most of them are located. Of course, we cannot neglect those unreached people groups whose countries, by accident of geography, just happen to lie outside the 10/40 Window. I call these the "9/41" peoples. We must remember that the 10/40 Window is just a helpful phrase. There is nothing sacred about it and there is nothing "extra special" or "super spiritual" about mission activity within it. But it is certainly a very helpful way to view the tremendous job still awaiting Christians today: reaching the remaining 7,000 unreached people groups of our world.

I hope that by now you are convinced that the Great Commission given by Jesus to His disciples is not yet fulfilled. Some of you, however, may be saying, "All this talk about people groups and unreached people groups sounds nice, but is it really biblical?" That's another good question. Is all this people group talk just a modern-day invention or is this a concept that is truly at the very center of God's heart throughout all time? In the next chapter we'll look in the Bible and find out.

INSIGHT:

Birth and death in the 10/40 window

We've already seen that most of the world's unreached peoples live in the area bordered by the 10/40 Window. I don't know about you, but I am overwhelmed by the huge number of people — literally millions upon millions — living in the Window. It is easier for me to grasp the reality of the people contained in the Window by looking instead at the number who are born and die there each day.[4]

Each and every day about 140,000 babies are born in the 10/40 Window countries. That works out to some

> 6,000 children born every hour,
> 100 each minute,
> 2 each second.

On the other side of the coin, each and every day some 58,000 individuals die in the 10/40 Window countries. And remember, most of those who die in that area of the world have never heard the Good News of Jesus. That means:

> 2,400 people from the 10/40 Window die and go to a Christless eternity every hour,
> 40 each minute, almost one every second.

In the time it takes you to read this very sentence five people have died, forever lost, and sixteen have been born and will soon need to hear a new presentation of the Gospel.

Is the command of Jesus in Matthew 28:19 already fulfilled? Not by a long shot.

---

4 These birth and death figures have been extrapolated from the estimates of the Worldometers website at www.worldometers.info.

Questions to think about

1   Take your Bible and look at the Great Commission of Jesus found in Matthew 28:16–20. Did Jesus give His Great Commission only to His first-century disciples, or to all Christians for all time? If the Great Commission is indeed for all of us, what is the implication of this for your life?

2   Can you think of any unreached people groups (or individuals from such groups) in your country or city? What can you or your church do to try to reach them?

3   At least twenty-five people die every minute without having had the chance to hear about Jesus Christ even once. How do you feel about this? What do you intend to do about it?

chapter two

PEOPLE GROUPS:
ALWAYS
ON GOD'S HEART

"There before me was a great multitude that no one could count,
from every nation, tribe, people and language . . ."
REVELATION 7:9

DOES GOD REALLY CARE?

The Early Christians did their homework!
The statistics presented in the last chapter show us that there are many people groups in the world today. In fact, there are over 17,000 of them. The exciting news is that Christians during the last 2,000 years have dutifully carried out their assignment from Jesus, the assignment He gave to His disciples in the Great Commission. Remember? Jesus commanded them to "Go and make disciples of all nations." By the providence of God the disciples were faithful to this Commission, and so in turn were millions of other Christians down through the last twenty centuries. And it's a good thing that they were faithful! Why? Because you and I probably would not be Christians today if it were not for the faithfulness of Christians who lived before us.

Think about it. If the Early Church really believed that the Great Commission was just for the first disciples of Jesus, then what would have happened? The Early Church probably would have become very ingrown and could have died out within a few generations. The Good News of Jesus would not be Good News for us because we would never have heard it. But, thank God, the Early Church — and those Christians who followed after — believed that Jesus' Great Commission was for all Christians. They believed it so seriously that today *some 10,000 people groups have already been reached with the Gospel of Jesus Christ. There are only 7,000 more groups to go* . . . and the exciting thing is that you and I get to be a part of reaching them!

"Hold on!" you say. "Not quite so fast."

Good point. I don't want to get you too excited about missions and reaching unreached people groups before I lay out some of the biblical evidence. After all, *the truly exciting part about missions is that people groups have been on God's heart throughout all time and eternity.* The Bible is full of God's concern to reach the peoples[1] of His world. It's time to make a quick survey of the Bible to seek out God's heart.

Let's begin at the beginning

Starting at the beginning is always a good idea. In the Bible, of course, the beginning is the book of Genesis. In the first eleven chapters of Genesis are found four major events: the sin of Adam and Eve; the slaying of Abel by Cain; the Flood, and Noah; and the building of the Tower of Babel. In each of these four events the major characters start out well but end up in sin.

Adam and Eve — the high point of God's creative act — follow temptation, and sin against their Creator. Now I don't know about you, but if I were God I would have smashed Adam and Eve and started all over again. But God, in His wisdom, did not do that. Yes, their sin had consequences (expulsion from the Garden, among

---

[1] In this chapter I use the words "peoples" and "people groups" interchangeably.

other things) but they were not killed. God's grace was greater than their sin.

Likewise with Cain and Abel. Again, I would have smashed Cain for killing another human being. And once again, Cain's sin has its consequences (banishment) but he also is given God's grace through the mark of protection on his forehead.

We see sin again in the human race at the time of Noah. Now, finally, God does indeed want to smash them all. But what happens? The Bible says that "Noah found favor [read: grace] in the eyes of the LORD" (Genesis 6:8). God, in His grace, spares Noah, his family, and the animals, so that they may begin again.

The last main event in Genesis 1–11 involves the Tower of Babel. Here humankind — united in a common language and culture — desires to build "a tower that reaches to the heavens so that we may make a name for ourselves . . ." (Genesis 11:4). Their desire to make a name for themselves meant that they wanted to glory in themselves and their achievements, not in the true God. In fact, by building this high tower they wanted to show that they were on a level with God and equal to Him. But God intervened. You know the story. He came down and "confused the language of the whole world. From there the LORD scattered them over the face of the whole earth" (Genesis 11:9).

Where is God's grace in the Tower of Babel account? Sure, God didn't destroy the people as He did at the time of the Flood. So that's grace. But there is more to it than that. Through the scattering of this one people God prepares the stage for a new development in His great plan for all of humankind. The culmination of the Tower of Babel story, however, doesn't come until Genesis chapter 12 and the calling of Abraham.

Abraham: Blessed to be a blessing
Where is God's grace in the Tower of Babel story? The answer is found in Genesis chapter 12, verses 1–3:

> The LORD had said to Abram, "Leave your country, your people and your father's household and go to the land I will show you. I will make you into a great nation and I will bless you; I will make your name great, and you will be a blessing. I will bless those who bless you, and whoever curses you I will curse; and all peoples on earth will be blessed through you."

God speaks about blessing Abraham if he is obedient. As a result, when we think of Abraham — and of the nation Israel who descended from Abraham — we most often think of them in terms of their being blessed by God. But this is only half of the picture. God is not blessing Abraham just because Abraham is obedient to Him, although that is certainly true. God is blessing Abraham *so that he will be a blessing.*

And just who is Abraham supposed to bless? The second half of verse three makes this clear: "and all peoples on earth will be blessed through you." Did you catch that? It's so important that I am going to repeat it. God says that the blessed Abraham will be a blessing to all peoples on earth. And who are all these peoples? They are the peoples who had previously been scattered at the Tower of Babel. At Babel God took one unified people, confused their common language, and made them many scattered peoples, each with a different language. Now through the one man Abraham — and his descendants who would include the nation Israel, and, eventually, God's own Son Jesus Christ — God reveals His heart and His plan. God's heart is for all of those scattered peoples. His plan is for one people to reach all of these other peoples. Thus we find the grace of God in the Tower of Babel story finally worked out through the life of Abraham. Remember this:

> Abraham and his descendants *were not blessed just to be blessed.* Rather, they *were blessed for a purpose: to be a blessing* to all those scattered peoples from the Tower of Babel.

Israel: Blessed to be a blessing

We have seen that God's heart, right from the very beginning of the Old Testament, is a heart full of wanting to reach all peoples. And His plan for reaching them all was to take one people — Israel — and bless them so that they, in turn, would be a blessing to the other peoples around them. In other words, God intended to bless Israel so much that the other peoples around her would sit up and take notice. These other peoples would then ask about this God who was blessing Israel.

As a result, they would also want to believe in, obey, and worship Israel's true God.

Unfortunately, it seldom worked out this way. Why? Because most of the time the people of Israel disobeyed God. Their sinfulness got in the way of their being able to be blessed or to be a blessing. This, however, was not God's original intention for them. More than anything else God wanted to bless them so that they, too, could be a blessing.

At no time was this made more clear than during the reigns of King David and his son Solomon. This period was the high point of Israel's history. The promise of God to bless Israel reached its peak during this time. Israel was one of the most powerful nations on earth and talk of the grandeur of Jerusalem and its temple and palace spread throughout the world. Israel was indeed blessed.

But David never forgot the reason why Israel was being blessed in the first place. He fully understood the fact that God was blessing them so that they, in turn, could be a blessing to the rest of the peoples and nations of the world. We can see this in David's (and Israel's) hymns — the Psalms — for which David primarily was responsible. There are some seventy-six references in the Psalms to the "nations." These, together with the many references to "peoples" and "all the earth," make it clear that during this time Israel worshiped God as the God of the entire world. Through the singing of these Psalms in the temple Israel was constantly reminded of why God was blessing her.

Psalm 67, in particular, beautifully reflects Israel's understanding that she was blessed to be a blessing. Here are the first three verses:

> May God be gracious to us and bless us
> and make his face shine upon us,
> that your ways may be known on earth,
> your salvation among all nations.
> May the peoples praise you, O God;
> may all the peoples praise you.

Israel was blessed to be a blessing. Why? So that all the peoples of the world might know about the true God whom Israel worshiped. This was and is the desire of God's heart, a heart not just for Abraham, not just for Israel, but a heart for all the peoples of the earth.

Jesus didn't change God's purpose

As we have seen in the Old Testament, Jesus' Father had a heart for all the peoples of the world whom He had created. What about His Son? Did Jesus, too, carry this same burden? Though Jesus' ministry was to the people of Israel, He very closely followed the original plan of His Father. He brought the Good News first of all to the Jews so that they, in turn, could bring this same Good News to all the peoples of the earth. The Great Commission given by Jesus, found in Matthew 28:19–20, makes this evident.

In these verses we read:

> Therefore go and make disciples of all nations, baptizing them in the name of the Father and of the Son and of the Holy Spirit, and teaching them to obey everything I have commanded you. And surely I am with you always, to the very end of the age.

In some of His last words to His followers — and to us today who claim to be His followers — Jesus gives the command to make disciples. But from what group of people should these disciples be made? From the Jews only? No, these disciples are to be made of all nations.

The phrase, "of all nations," is very significant. Jesus' use of the word "nations" is not the same as our use of the word today. Jesus speaks with a different emphasis. How so? The Greek words used in the phrase, "of all nations," are *panta ta ethne*. The word *ethne* is where, in English, we get the word "ethnic." The word refers to different ethnic groups, or people groups. Jesus is not saying that we are to make disciples of all the *nations* of the world, geographical and physical entities — like the Philippines or the United States or Japan — although we can indeed expect to see disciples in heaven from every nation. Rather:

> Jesus is commanding His followers, both then and now, to make disciples of all the *ethnic people groups* found within all of the countries of the world.

Today, this means reaching 7,000 yet-to-be-reached unreached people groups. So Jesus is very clearly carrying on the original plan of His Father. His heart's concern is also for all of the peoples of the world.

The Early Church keeps it going
The first disciples of Jesus, and the Early Church, aggressively carried out Jesus' Great Commission. Beginning where they were, in Jerusalem, they carried the Good News of Jesus to different peoples in Jerusalem, Judea, Samaria and the ends of the earth (see Acts 1:8). They kept central in their own lives and ministries God's concern for the people groups of the world.

Nowhere is this better demonstrated than in the life and ministry of the Apostle Paul. Paul is the best New Testament example of someone who also had a heart for peoples. This can be seen in many places in Paul's speeches and writings (Acts 13: 46–47; Romans 4:16–17, 15:7–12; and Galatians 3:6–9). It is especially found towards the end of his letter to the Romans:

I will not venture to speak of anything except what Christ has accomplished through me in leading the Gentiles to obey God by what I have said and done — by the power of signs and miracles, through the power of the Spirit. So from Jerusalem all the way around to Illyricum, I have fully proclaimed the gospel of Christ. It has always been my ambition to preach the gospel where Christ was not known, so that I would not be building on someone else's foundation. Rather, as it is written:

"Those who were not told about him will see, and those who have not heard will understand," (Romans 15:18–21).

Paul could have easily spent the rest of his life traveling throughout the regions he had already visited. Certainly the large area "from Jerusalem all the way around to Illyricum" — a great arc extending from Judea to Italy — still needed lots of evangelistic work and follow-up. Why then did Paul want to move on? John Piper writes that because of Paul's heart for all the peoples of the world:

. . . Paul's conception of the missionary task is not merely the winning of more and more people to Christ (which he could have done very efficiently in these familiar regions), but the reaching of more and more peoples or nations. His focus was not primarily on new geographic areas. Rather he was gripped by the vision of unreached peoples.[2]

Clearly Paul's heart beat in rhythm with God's heart. In his missionary journeys he helped the Early Church keep the Great Commission of Jesus urgent and alive.

---

[2] From John Piper, *Let the Nations Be Glad! The Supremacy of God in Missions*, 3rd edition, 2010. Grand Rapids, MI: Baker, p. 203.

Good News! We win!

When we talk about bringing God's Good News to all of the remaining unreached people groups in the world — 7,000 of them — it would be easy to become discouraged. Sure, the desire of God's heart is to reach them all. But . . . can we really do it? In human terms the task looks impossible. But do you know what? It's going to happen! The very last book of the Bible makes this abundantly clear.

In the book of Revelation, chapter 7, verses 9–10, John describes what is going to happen at the very end of the age, at the very end of time. John says:

> After this I looked and there before me was a great multitude that no one could count, from every nation, tribe, people and language, standing before the throne and in front of the Lamb. They were wearing white robes and were holding palm branches in their hands. And they cried out in a loud voice: "Salvation belongs to our God, who sits on the throne, and to the Lamb."

Isn't that exciting! *At the end of the world there will indeed be individuals who are Christians from every single people group in the world.* All the *ethnes* who have ever lived will have at least one representative worshiping God in Heaven. We are going to win! All the peoples of the world will be evangelized! What God first promised to Abraham will one day fully come to pass.

Conclusion

That was a quick overview of missions in the Bible. But it gives enough biblical evidence to prove that God's heart — right from the very beginning — has been a heart for the peoples of the world. He wants all the scattered people groups of the earth to hear the Gospel of Jesus Christ. He wants all the unreached people groups of the world to accept His Son Jesus as Savior and Lord. Is this the responsibility of professional evangelists and missionaries alone? No, I've got bad news for you if you think that. The responsibility is for *every Christian*. It's not a question of *if* God wants to use you to help bless the peoples of the world, even today; it's a question of *how*. How does God want to use you? We turn to that question in the next chapter.

ACTS 1:8
A stumbling block for missions?

I believe that a wrong understanding of Acts 1:8 has prevented more Christians from becoming missionaries than any other verse in the Bible. Why? The verse is so familiar: "And you will be my witnesses in Jerusalem, and in all Judea and Samaria, and to the ends of the earth." Unfortunately, because it is so familiar we neglect to examine it carefully.

What do I mean? Most interpret the verse like this: Jerusalem refers to my own family, friends, and home town; Judea refers to my county, region or state; Samaria refers to the next region or state, or to the borders of my country; and the "ends of the earth" refers to just that, going to places outside of my own country. As a result, most Christians think that "Real missions work" doesn't begin until someone goes to "the ends of the earth."

Why is this common interpretation wrong? It has to do with geography. Look at the maps found at the back of your Bible. Find two places: Nazareth and Jerusalem. Now ask yourself these two questions: Where was the disciples' home town? and Where were the disciples when Jesus said these words in Acts 1:8?

The answers? Firstly, **Jerusalem was not the disciples' home town.** The disciples were "small town boys," mainly fishermen from Galilee. Whenever they did go to Jerusalem they were always recognized as being different (Matthew 26:73 and Acts 2:7). When Jesus commanded the disciples to begin first in Jerusalem, he was commanding them **from the very**

31

beginning of their ministry to be involved in a type of cross-cultural work **among peoples different from themselves!**

I'm sure that the disciples would have much preferred going back to their homes, families and friends up in Galilee, beginning to spread Christianity from there. But God had a better idea.

God's better idea is quickly revealed in the very next chapter of Acts when "Jews from every nation under heaven" (Acts 2:6, and verses 8–12) hear Peter's Pentecost speech, and 3,000 of them believe and are baptized that very day (Acts 2:41).

The disciples willingly shared the Gospel with all these Jews who were culturally different from themselves. What better way can you imagine to spread the Good News of Jesus throughout the world than for these converted Jews to return to their home towns, after Pentecost, taking the Gospel to all the people groups where they live? What better location than Jerusalem can you imagine as a starting point for a God concerned for all peoples to begin to spread Christianity! But it would never have happened if the original disciples had interpreted Acts 1:8 as many do today, and responded by returning immediately to their home towns in Galilee, witnessing for the rest of their lives only to their families and friends.

What's the significance of all of this? We cannot excuse ourselves any longer from seriously considering cross-cultural missions among the unreached peoples of this world, saying that we feel that God has called us first to be witnesses to our families and friends in our own "home town" Jerusalems. That is precisely why this verse has been such a stumbling block to missions over the years. Christians have been too comfortable interpreting this verse in a way that enables them to avoid ever considering cross-cultural missions in the first place. Too many Christians have responded like this: "God has called me to my 'Jerusalem': my family and friends and home town. That's all."

God may indeed restrict you to this legitimate ministry, but not on the basis of Acts 1:8. Rather, in Acts 1:8 Jesus is telling His disciples — and all Christians today who call themselves His disciples — that we must minister for Jesus to people who may be different from us **right where we are**. This verse commands us to reach out to those peoples different from ourselves in whose midst God, in His sovereignty, has placed us. We reach out first **where we are**. Then we reach out to peoples in places near and far.

God is a God whose heart is concerned for all peoples. Acts chapter 1, verse 8, is but another example of His global concern.

Questions to think about

1   What would you have done if you were God, observing the events of Genesis 1–11? How do you think God looks upon some of the things that happen in the world today? How does God's grace come through even today?

2   Explain how God's choice to bless one people — Abraham and his descendants, the nation Israel — is really a part of His grand plan to bless all peoples, all nations.

3   Look carefully at Acts 1:8. How did you once interpret this verse? How will you interpret it now, especially in relation to your own life?

4   In heaven there will be at least one person from every single people group on the face of the earth. How does this truth from the book of Revelation make you feel? Why?

chapter three

SO WHAT ARE YOU GOING TO DO ABOUT IT?

"The harvest is plentiful but the workers are few. Ask the Lord of the harvest, therefore, to send out workers into his harvest field."
MATTHEW 9:37–38

WHO, ME?

All Christians must make a decision
In the last chapter we saw how the entire Bible gives evidence that the desire of God's heart is to reach all the peoples of the world. The biblical account shows that God purposefully planned to reach all the peoples through one people, Israel, and that this plan culminated in His Son, Jesus Christ. Furthermore, the evidence of the Bible shows that this plan is passed on to all who claim to be followers of Jesus. This was true for those who followed Jesus in the New Testament times and is still true for those who follow Him today. This is the really exciting part!

Why? Because God, in His providence, has allowed *you and me* the privilege of playing a small part in helping to reach the remaining unreached people groups of this world. We, like the Apostle Paul, can have hearts that beat with the rhythm of God's heart.

How do we make our hearts beat with the rhythm of God's heart? Quite simply, we must consciously make the decision to be obedient to the Great Commission. The decision comes down to this:

> If Jesus commanded all of us to make disciples of all of the peole groups of the world, then *what are we going to do about it?*

Yes, indeed, what are you going to do about it? What am I going to do about it? This question hits us right between the eyes. We can avoid it no longer.

For you see, if we are truly followers of Jesus Christ then we have to take His Great Commission seriously. And if we take it seriously then we only have one choice. The choice is this:

> To help send others to make disciples of all the people groups, or . . . to be sent out to do it ourselves.

That's all. It's very simple. Either we help send others or we get ourselves sent out. Both options are obedient to the Great Commission. We go or we help others so that they might go. There are no other choices. We have to make a decision. Now.

Why a decision needs to be made:
The Great Imbalance

Can't we avoid it? Can't we put off the decision just a little bit longer? No! We can't, because if we do then the unreached peoples of this world will remain unreached. Look at the facts. Today in the world there are approximately 400,000 Protestant missionaries.[1]

---

[1] Figures used here are taken from "Missions Stats" found at www.thetravelingteam.org/stats

This figure includes both Western and non-Western missionaries.

Some of you are probably thinking: "What a large figure! With 400,000 missionaries surely the job of reaching the world's unreached peoples is almost done. Maybe I won't have to make a decision concerning the Great Commission after all."

Wrong! Why is this thinking wrong? Because unfortunately, at best, only some 20,000 of these 400,000 missionaries are actually working among unreached people groups. There is a great imbalance in the deployment of the world's missionary force. And this great imbalance explains why the job of reaching the world's unreached peoples is still such a large task. Look carefully below at what I call, "The Great Imbalance Seesaw."

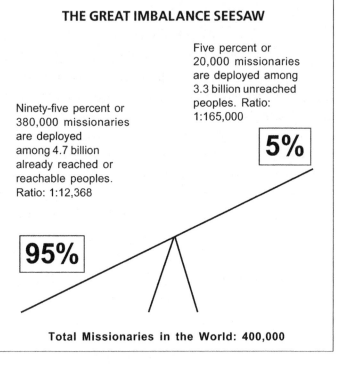

THE GREAT IMBALANCE SEESAW

Five percent or 20,000 missionaries are deployed among 3.3 billion unreached peoples. Ratio: 1:165,000

5%

Ninety-five percent or 380,000 missionaries are deployed among 4.7 billion already reached or reachable peoples. Ratio: 1:12,368

95%

Total Missionaries in the World: 400,000

By examining THE GREAT IMBALANCE SEESAW we find that the reached or reachable people groups have approximately 380,000 of all the missionaries in the world working among them.

"OK," some of you may be saying. "So most of the world's population has most of the world's missionaries, so what?"

So what? The point is that this means that ninety-five percent of the world's missionaries are working among people groups that are already reached or who can be reached by the existing Christians and churches that are already found among them. With 380,000 missionaries there *is one missionary for every 12,368 already reached or reachable individuals.*

By contrast, the unreached peoples of the world make up 3.3 billion of the world's population but currently have only some 20,000 — a mere five percent — of the world's total missionary personnel. This works out to a ratio of *one missionary for every 165,000 individuals in unreached people groups.*

The contrast is striking: ninety-five percent or 380,000 missionaries compared with five percent or 20,000 missionaries. What a contrast! What an imbalance!

Some of you may have played on a seesaw when you were a child. Remember how the big bully would sit with all of his weight on the bottom of the seesaw and leave you hanging on for dear life at the top? Well, we can't take that analogy too far but it somewhat represents the current state of affairs in relation to the deployment of the world's missionary force. The seesaw is weighted in favor of those people groups who are already reached or reachable. Most of the people groups who are still unreached are being left to themselves.

What can we do about this great imbalance? Some missions experts estimate that we need at least 100,000 new missionaries to effectively reach the remaining unreached people groups of our world.[2] We can't just relocate the 380,000 missionaries who are now working

---

[2] The need for at least 100,000 new missionaries for unreached people groups is a low-end estimate. Some missions experts are calling for at least 200,000 new missionaries, some as many as one million. Whatever is the final best estimate, it is clear that the need for many new missionaries to the unreached people groups is urgent.

among reached and reachable people groups. Why not? Because most of them are currently involved in important missions-related ministries. So that means we need

100,000 *new* missionaries

for the remaining 7,000 unreached people groups! This works out to about fifteen new missionaries for each unreached group. For some of the smaller groups, this will be enough, but for those unreached groups that number in the millions there will be a lot more missionaries needed than just fifteen per group.

What about you? Does God want you to be one of these 100,000? Or does He want you actively involved in helping to *send out* several of these 100,000? Of course, you may instead choose to join the ranks of the 380,000 regular missionaries or to help send out more regular missionaries. Either way — whether in relation to the call for 100,000 new missionaries to unreached peoples or the call for more regular missionaries — a choice about your involvement needs to be made. What will your decision be?

There is nothing "super Christian" or "super spiritual" about either going or sending. There is no hierarchy of spiritual gifts in God's Kingdom. "Sent ones" are not better than "senders." Remember this:

> Both "senders" and "sent ones" are of equal importance for the furtherance of God's Kingdom among unreached peoples.

I say this because, unfortunately, the "sent out" missionaries are oftentimes put high up on spiritual pedestals. They are seen in many Christian circles as premier Christians. Now don't get me wrong. Many missionaries are indeed specially gifted people and they should be given honor and respect. However, we must realize that the sending gifts are just as important. Without good senders, the "sent out" missionaries will not have adequate prayer support and financial resources to do their jobs. If you feel that God is leading you to a sending role, praise the Lord! You will want to give the best possible effort you can to assist others in reaching the unreached peoples of this world. Don't for a minute consider yourself inferior or "second class." Your role is crucial.

If, on the other hand, you feel that God is leading you to be sent out as a missionary to the unreached peoples, again, praise the Lord! You are urgently needed. But always remember that you are not any better than those who remain behind in the more supportive sending role.

Remember the choices. We go, or we help others so they might go. Those of us who call ourselves disciples of Jesus need to seriously grapple with the choice that needs to be made. But don't be too hasty with your decision. You will want to carefully discern God's will. As you read your Bible and as you pray, ask God to give you specific direction. Remember, He has a lot more riding on your decision than you do. He wants to help you to make the decision that is according to His will. It would be nice to receive a gold-embossed letter in the mail from heaven — special delivery direct from God — telling you exactly what you are supposed to do. Sorry, but God doesn't work that way. *He will* answer you. Just be patient. Always keep this in mind:

> God will guide you to the proper decision but only as you seek His direction.

There are many things to consider with each choice. We're going to look at some of them in the next two chapters. In Chapter Four we will deal with some of the issues that concern those who feel that God is directing them to be obedient to the Great Commission *through sending others*. In Chapter Five we will deal with those who feel that God is directing them to be obedient to the Great Commission *through going themselves as "sent ones."*

Be sure to read *both* chapters. Why? Because if you are a "sent one" you will want to know about some of the qualities and prerequisites necessary for those Christians whom you want on your sending team. And for you "senders," you will want to look at some of the qualities and prerequisites necessary for those Christians whom you will actually help to "send out." We'll look first, in Chapter Four, at those who send.

Missions: Where do I fit in?

Many of you are trying to determine God's will for your life in relationship to the Great Commission. Here are ten helpful questions to ask yourself to see where you might fit in.

1 **For what part of the world do I have an interest or burden?** From the time you were a small child you may have had a special twinge inside whenever you heard of a certain country or people group. Could that feeling be from God?

2 **What has God already spoken to me about missions?** God rarely uses lightning strikes to convince somebody to become a missionary. Instead He uses His "still small voice" that gently leads us towards doing His will. It is important to not only listen for that small voice but to be obedient to it.

3 **What type of missions ministry might I fit into?** Greg Livingston, the founder of Frontiers — now with over 1,000 missionaries among Muslim peoples — says this: Don't ask if you are the missionary type; instead ask how the gifts, abilities or skills that you already have can be used on a church planting team.

4 **What do others say are my gifts, abilities and skills?** It is always a good thing to know what are your gifts, abilities or skills, especially if you might be considering missions. Believe it or not, God can use just about anybody as long as they are willing to be obedient to Him.

5 **What is my "calling"? How does this sense of a calling relate to my gifts, abilities and skills?** Not everyone is called to be a Billy Graham or a William Carey. It's important to match your calling with those gifts, abilities or skills of which you are already aware. Nothing magically happens once you board the airplane, train or boat bound for the missions field. Start by using what you have. It's what God gave you.

6 **Do I have any negative attitudes toward people of other races/cultures?** Negative attitudes don't miraculously disappear once a missionary gets to the missions field. All Christians need to work on these negative attitudes, but especially potential missionaries. If these negative attitudes are too strong you may not really be a good missionary candidate.

7 **How soon should I go into missions service?** Yes, over 50,000 individuals die every day without hearing a credible presentation of the Gospel. But that still doesn't mean you don't need adequate preparation. God took eighty years to prepare Moses and thirteen years or so to prepare the apostle Paul. Certainly a year or two of good preparation in your own life is not too much to invest. And you will be much more effective as a result.

8 **If God clearly shows that missionary service is not for me, then how can I get more involved in helping those who are ministering among the unreached peoples?** Not everyone is sent to the unreached peoples. But every Christian can be a good sender of others who are sent for such a task. How can you be a better prayer, supporter, and giver of money for those who are sent out?

9 **What are my fears?** It's good to be honest about the task of missions. Being a missionary among unreached peoples can be one of the toughest jobs in the world. But in my opinion it is among the most rewarding jobs as well. So acknowledge your fears as real and legitimate, and then deal with them with God's help.

10 **What are my dreams?** Dream big dreams for God! Want to reach an unreached people group with the Gospel? Want to see them one day worshipping together with you at the throne of God? Nothing is impossible with God's help! And remember, He loves to give us the desires of our hearts.

Questions to think about

1   How does "The Great Imbalance" in the number of missionaries to reached and unreached peoples make you feel? What are you going to do about it?

2   Why are those who send and those who are sent both vital in reaching the unreached peoples of our world?

3   What decision have you made concerning the Great Commission and where you might fit in? Share your decision with your pastor and/or another good Christian friend. Be sure to have them pray for you and for your decision.

chapter four

FOR YOU WHO SEND OTHERS

"And how can they preach unless they are sent?"
ROMANS 10:15

WHAT CAN YOU DO?

Senders in the New Testament Church

As we saw in the previous chapter, all Christians who want to be obedient to Jesus Christ and His Great Commission have to make a decision. We must decide between sending others or being sent ourselves. Many of you have already decided that God is directing you to help send others out to the missions field. Some of you are still trying to discover God's will concerning this matter. Others of you feel God prompting you to go yourselves, and you want to identify some key elements necessary for building a good sending team. Whatever your present situation may be, it is important to realize that senders have always played a major role in missions from the very beginnings of Christianity. From the book of Acts, and throughout the history of the Church, senders have been indispensable. Let's look at some examples.

We find evidence of the first missionary sending team early in the development of the New Testament church. In Acts 13:1–3 we read:

> In the church at Antioch there were prophets and
> teachers: Barnabas, Simeon called Niger, Lucius

of Cyrene, Manaen . . . and Saul. While they were worshiping the Lord and fasting, the Holy Spirit said, "Set apart for me Barnabas and Saul for the work to which I have called them." So after they had fasted and prayed, they placed their hands on them and sent them off.

These five men modeled the essentials of any missionary team. How? Three of them became the "senders" and two became the "sent ones." God did not direct Barnabas and Saul (Paul) to go to the mission field all by themselves. Instead God directed them *in the context of the missionary sending team* of Simeon, Lucius, and Manaen. Of course, these "senders" also represented the entire Antioch church (see Acts 14:26–27), yet these three were the chief ones who made up the missionary sending team of Barnabas and Paul.

The Apostle Paul recognized the important role of senders to missions, probably because of his own intimate contact with these three special senders from his home church in Antioch. Here's what he writes in Romans 10:14–15a:

How, then, can they call on the one they have not believed in? And how can they believe in the one of whom they have not heard? And how can they hear without someone preaching to them? And how can they preach unless they are sent?

Paul here sees a direct relationship between those sent to proclaim the Gospel and those who send. Paul describes the relationship: calling upon Jesus is built on belief, which is built on hearing, which is built on preaching, which is built on sending. Sending, then, forms the foundation of the entire process, as represented by the diagram below:

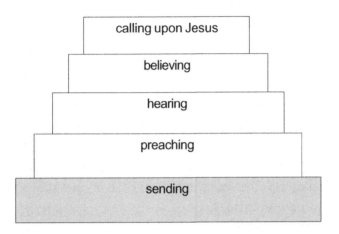

Paul's ministry was made possible by his sending church in Antioch, and especially by his missionary sending team. Paul and the Antioch church had a special relationship throughout his missionary career. At the beginning of each of his three missionary journeys Paul leaves from his home church in Antioch (Acts 13:1, 15:35, and 18:23). When he returns from his first and second missionary journeys he goes first to the Antioch church to show his Powerpoint and video presentations (!) and to give his report (Acts 14:27 and 18:22). From his writing and from his actions we see clearly that, for Paul, the senders in the Antioch church were crucial to the success of his ministry.

Senders throughout history

Senders, like those in the Antioch church, continued to play important roles in the growth of the Church during the twenty centuries from the New Testament times to today. I have chosen three more groups of senders from this long history for us to consider together.

Let's look first at the monks of the early Middle Ages. Many of us today think of monasteries as places where priests and nuns go to get away from the world. This understanding, however, is not necessarily accurate. During the thousand year period AD 500–AD 1500, from the time of the Middle Ages to the Reformation, missionaries were sent out primarily by the monasteries. Monasteries became the central base of operations for new mission thrusts.

For example, in the sixth century the Irish monk, Columba, established networks of Irish monasteries that became the headquarters for a variety of missionary activities. He journeyed north from Ireland to the island of Iona, off the west coast of Scotland. From this base he established a chain of monasteries across Scotland that evangelized the various unreached Scottish peoples. Another Irish monk by the name of Columbanus repeated the pattern of his namesake. With twelve fellow monks he went from Ireland to the European continent and eventually to the unreached people group known as the Franks who lived in eastern France. Wherever he went, like Columba, he also established monasteries as centers for missionary sending activity.

Why the success of these Irish missionaries and the thousands of others like them? Because, by God's grace, both the financial and prayer support necessary for their missionary endeavors was provided by the monastic system. The sending monks who remained back in the monasteries played key roles in the reaching of many European unreached people groups.

Next, let's look at a small group of Christians who lived during the early eighteenth century. This Moravian group was composed of religious refugees who eventually settled down in Germany on the land of a man named Count Ludwig von Zinzendorf. Zinzendorf was no ordinary Count. Rather, he was a Count with a passion to reach unreached peoples with the Gospel. Through his leadership this group of Moravians was transformed into a major missionary movement. A few individuals from this small group were sent to the West Indies in 1732, and in the course of the next twenty-eight years the Moravians sent missionaries to twenty-eight different countries. By the time of Zinzendorf's death in 1760 the Moravians had sent out two hundred and twenty-six missionaries. At the height of their missionary zeal they were sending out one missionary for every ten senders who stayed behind at home in Germany!

Our last example concerns the United States. In the late nineteenth century, there was a huge revival of missions interest in the churches. It was very much like what is happening in many parts of the world today, but this particular revival was among students, giving rise to what was called the Student Volunteer Movement. Beginning in 1886, the Movement sent out some twenty thousand missionaries over the next fifty years. But just as important as this impressive number of *sent missionaries* was the huge number of *senders* who stayed behind and consistently gave financial and prayer support for those who went. How many were committed to this important sending task? Some *eighty thousand*! And the world is still feeling the positive effect of these twenty thousand Student Volunteers because of the eighty thousand back home who sent them out with power.

Some guidelines for those who send others
What do the missions efforts of the Antioch church, the monasteries of the Middle Ages, the Moravians and the Student Volunteer Movement all have in common? They all centered upon key groups of senders whose fundamental goal in life was to support missionaries sent from their various communities. This same kind of motivation is necessary in the lives of senders today.

"What?" you may ask. "Does this mean that I must live my life like the monks or the Moravians in order to be a good sender?" No, not necessarily. Though the monks, Moravians and other senders throughout Church history may indeed be good role models for senders today, it does not mean that their lifestyles necessarily would be appropriate for senders in the twenty-first century. However, we can learn much from these senders of the past, especially as we observe one element that characterized the lives of them all. What was this element? It was their primary motivation in life: a zeal for missions and for the sending of missionaries so that the Gospel would penetrate to the very ends of the earth. This was their overwhelming passion. It is this zeal that today's senders can and should attempt to duplicate. All who would be senders ought to remember this:

> A zeal for missions and for missionaries is foundational for those who send.

How this zeal is worked out in each sender's life will vary. There is no set formula. You will have to develop a sending lifestyle that you are comfortable with. But your underlying zeal for those whom you send — and for their ministries — is vital, no matter how you may choose to live your life.

Two key responsibilities for senders

If God leads you to make the decision to stay so that you may help send others, then it is important for you to see the tremendous responsibility — and privilege — that is yours in two primary areas. Of course, there are many other important areas where you may also be of sending assistance. But these two are crucial in getting your missionary to the field and keeping him or her there.

Responsibility No.1: FINANCIAL SUPPORT

Missions involves money. There is no way around this fact. Regardless of where they are from or where they are going — missionaries need financial support. Salaries, adequate health insurance, work funds, vehicle or transportation funds, children's education, Social Security, travel to and from the area of service, retirement — the list of potential financial needs goes on and on. Most of these items, and more, will be a part of the financial needs of your missionaries and their ministries.

So what are you, as a sender, going to do about it? First, remember that many missionaries are reluctant to talk about their financial needs. Why? Because oftentimes they know that their friends and churches already have tremendous financial obligations. To ask friends and churches to take on even more financial responsibility seems inappropriate. So how can you help your missionary talk about money? Right from the beginning make your missionary comfortable with talking about his or her financial needs. You be the one to ask questions about their support needs. By bringing finances out into the open yourself you free your missionary to talk about the reality of his or her financial needs.

Being a sender means that you will personally help meet the financial responsibilities of your missionaries. There is no way around the fact that if you are going to help fulfill the Great Commission you are going to have to give a significant percentage of your money for missions. How much money? The answer to that question will vary, depending on your financial obligations and resources. You will need to prayerfully seek God's will concerning how much to give and to whom. Some senders may opt for a simple lifestyle giving any excess money and time for missions. Other senders may choose to be successful in the business world or in another professional sphere so that the money they make may be used to support missionaries. There is no single ideal.

It may be wise to limit yourself to giving bigger chunks for a few missionaries rather than giving smaller amounts to each of several missionaries. Why? Because it is much more difficult for the missionary who has to raise, for example, $20 per month from one hundred individuals, than to raise $100 per month from twenty individuals. And, of course, if your church or denomination has a strategic missions program, then you will also need to balance your support-giving between supporting individual missionaries that you personally commit to assist and helping to meet the overall financial responsibilities of your church or denomination. Remember, too, that you will need to periodically increase the amount of your monthly giving to your missionary, to keep up with the rising cost of missions due to inflation and other factors.

Responsibility No.2: PRAYER SUPPORT
Of course finances are important to those missionaries that you will help to send out. But more crucial even than financial support is prayer support. "Sure," many of you are saying, "everyone knows that prayer is important for missions." Yet, in spite of this knowledge, many Christians give only lip service to this important fact. What senders must realize is that their prayers

are vital for those missionaries whom they send out. Indeed, senders are directly engaged in a spiritual battle for the very souls of unreached peoples. The battle is oftentimes won or lost depending upon the fervent prayers of the senders back home. Missionaries are fully dependent upon this kind of praying.

Senders, you need to pray. And your prayers must move beyond — far beyond — the broad "God, please bless all the missionaries" prayers that are all too common. I call these prayers "shotgun" prayers. Why? Because a shotgun shoots out a lot of little pellets that may or may not hit some part of the target. Shotgun prayers, likewise, may or may not hit the target. Your prayers need to be "rifle prayers": prayers targeting specific people and needs and situations. How do you pray like this for the ones you send? By being intimately acquainted with the missionaries whom you send.

You can't pray specific rifle prayers for all the missionaries. That's an impossible task. You can, however, pray for a handful of carefully chosen missionaries whom God especially lays upon your heart. And for these you will pray consistently, daily or weekly. You will carefully read their prayer letters, email updates, or social media postings. You will faithfully correspond with them — through letter, email, or through social media — while they are on the field. You will meet with them often when they are home. Why will you do all of these things? So that you can more effectively pray for them, and for the people among whom they work. Then your prayers will be rifle prayers: fixing the target firmly in your sights and firing the prayer off to our Father in heaven.

So how can you begin doing this? Here's a suggestion. Band together with other like-minded senders, especially those who have a special concern for the same missionary or missionaries. Keep yourselves accountable to pray for your missionaries. This accountability should be for you as an individual as well as for you as a group. Get together regularly (once-a-week or once-a-month) for an extended time of prayer for your chosen missionaries. (This is also a good time to write them an e-mail letter, with each one of you jotting down an encouraging sentence or two.) At the same time keep your missionaries accountable to your group by requiring them to send periodic prayer requests and ministry updates (e-mail and social media makes this very easy). Why? Because you will need current information to be able to pray more intelligently. By banding together as a committed group you will soon be praying effective prayers for your missionaries. You will soon be rifle pray-ers. And Satan will be looking for refuge from your sharpshooting!

Some final cautions for those who would send others

Senders, do not take your sending responsibilities lightly! When missionaries are sent out today the emphasis in many churches is almost entirely upon those who are sent, with little consideration — or responsibility — put upon those who send. This is not as it should be. If all Christians are called upon by Jesus to help fulfill the Great Commission then it follows that *both "senders" and "sent ones" are equally responsible to the Lord for their role in reaching the unreached peoples of this world.*

Most Christians, unfortunately, have delegated their sending responsibilities to mission organizations. As a result, they feel little or no responsibility for either their church's missionaries or for the mission field. Now don't get me wrong. Mission organizations are vital to missions today. But the existence of missionary organizations should in no way diminish the financial and prayer responsibilities of individual Christians.

Senders, you are needed! Seldom before in the history of the Church has there been such a tremendous need for so many new missionaries doing frontline missionary work among unreached peoples. Seldom before in the history of the Church has the Holy Spirit been moving in such a mighty way in so many countries, and among so many unreached people groups, as He is today. It is incredibly exciting!

Don't get left out. Don't give your sending responsibilities away to the mission agencies. But even more importantly:

> Don't be a part of a sending team until you are willing to go *all the way* with the missionaries you send.

Why do I say this? Because working among many of these unreached peoples is difficult. Oftentimes today our churches are interested primarily in large numbers of converts and the planting of many churches. The missionaries doing this type of work are many times looked upon as the "most successful." Success among unreached peoples, however, cannot and should not be judged in this way. Sure, some of the unreached people groups are going to quickly respond by the hundreds and thousands to the Good News of Jesus Christ. However, other unreached groups — perhaps the majority of them — may take a longer time to reach. Conversions may be slow. Churches or fellowship groups may take many years to plant.

Are you ready for the long haul? Will you demand quick success of your missionaries rather than waiting patiently for God's work among their particular unreached people group? Are you ready and willing to give your chosen missionaries financial and prayer support for five years, ten years, twenty years, or more? Don't let the world's opinion of success, and its short attention span, be a part of your attitude towards your missionaries.

Jesus Himself admonishes all of us who would be His disciples to "count the cost" before committing ourselves to His service (see Luke 14:28–3). In like manner, senders must count the cost before committing themselves to be part of a missionary sending team. Are you ready to count the cost for your missionary? The missionary's responsibilities are difficult enough in the first place without their having to worry about whether or not their senders back home will stick it out with them through good times and bad. They critically need reliable, consistent, unfailing senders. Be that kind of a sender for your missionary. Be a sender who has counted the cost.

INSIGHT:

Senders and their prayers

This is the true story of a missionary and his wife who set out for Africa years ago. Before they left, the members of their home church promised to faithfully pray for them. Their confidence strengthened by this promise, the young missionaries courageously boarded a ship for the long trip to Africa. Sadly, within two years of their arrival the missionary's wife and his new baby died from an African disease. He himself succumbed to the disease and, having only months to live, sailed back unannounced to his home country.

He arrived back in his home town and on Wednesday evening this dying, broken man proceeded directly to the weekly prayer service that was held in his home church. Silently he seated himself at the back of the building and listened to the prayers.

At the end of the prayer meeting he got up and slowly made his way down the aisle to the front of the church. He turned to the astonished prayer group and this is what he said:

"I am your missionary. My wife and child are buried in Africa and I have come home to die. This evening I listened anxiously, as you prayed, for some mention of your missionary, to see if you were keeping your promise, but in vain! You prayed for everything connected with yourselves and your church, but you forgot your missionary. I see now why I am a failure as a missionary. It is because you have failed to hold the ropes!"[1]

---

[1] This story is adapted from Steve Murrel's "When Churches Don't Pray," *Victory Fire*, 2(4) July 43:26–27.

What can senders learn from this devastating story? The power of prayer is a real power. The need to pray for your missionaries is real. Those who are senders must not take this task lightly. The very lives of your missionaries may depend upon it. The effectiveness of their ministries depends upon it. More importantly, the eternal lives of individuals who make up the 7,000 unreached people groups are also dependent upon your faithfulness in praying.

Prayer is the number one responsibility of senders. It is very easy to agree to pray for someone, like the members of the church of the missionary sent to Africa. It is oftentimes a difficult task to actually pray the effective and consistent prayers that are so necessary for the success of the missionaries. Don't take this task lightly!

In fact, why not stop right now and pray for your missionaries? Renew the covenant that you made with them — perhaps sometime in the distant past — to pray consistently for them. Today is your opportunity to begin praying faithfully for them once again.

Questions to think about

1   Why does the Apostle Paul emphasize both "senders" and "sent ones"? What kind of relationship did Paul have with his own sending church? Is Paul's relationship a good model for missions today? Why or why not?

2   Were the problems of life faced by the monks, Moravians, and members of the Student Volunteer Movement any different from the problems that face Christians today? How do you think these past senders of missionaries were able to keep their missionary sending zeal focused?

3   For you who would be senders, why are financial and prayer support key factors in the sending of missionaries? In what ways can you be more effective in these areas? Have you counted the cost?

4   For you who would be sent, how will the discussion in this chapter influence you as you recruit a sending team?

chapter five

FOR YOU WHO ARE SENT

"Then I heard the voice of the Lord saying, 'Whom shall I send? And who will go for us?' And I said, 'Here am I. Send me!'"
ISAIAH 6:8

COULD THIS BE YOU?

First things first

In the last chapter we examined some factors to consider if you want to help fulfill the Great Commission by sending others to the mission field. Now it is time to examine some key factors for those of you who feel that God is directing you to be sent as a missionary yourself.

Before we go further, let me clarify something. In this chapter I am not merely challenging you to become a "regular" missionary. (By "regular" missionary I mean one who desires to minister among already-reached or reachable people groups.) Though this type of worker will still be needed on the mission field in the future, what I say here, by-and-large, is not for this type of missionary.

Why not? Because, in Chapter Three, we learned that the world already has some 380,000 "regular" missionaries who are ministering among reached or reachable people groups. Remember? In that chapter we also learned that there are only some 20,000 missionaries to unreached people groups and that there is a need for at least 100,000 more. Think of them as "frontier" or "pioneer" missionaries. Yes, regular missionaries are still needed, but I am writing here to men and women urgently needed as "frontier" missionaries to minister among the unreached peoples of this world. Frontier missionaries are a rare breed today: men and women able and willing to be on the front lines of unreached peoples' work, directly involved in cross-cultural evangelism and church planting in a culture where Christ is not yet known.

In this chapter I also address those of you who may feel God leading you to be involved *indirectly* among unreached peoples. What do I mean by "indirectly"? I mean that some of you may be qualified to help *train* others, especially in the non-Western world, others who will in turn serve as missionaries to unreached peoples. The *training* of missionaries to unreached peoples is an important ministry, and will continue to be for the foreseeable future.

Since "sent ones" and the "trainers of sent ones" share several overlapping concerns, I write to you both in this chapter. First, we will look briefly at factors affecting those who will train others to reach unreached peoples. Then the bulk of the chapter will zero in on considerations for those of you who hope to be sent as cross-cultural frontier missionaries to one of the 7,000 unreached people groups.

For those who are sent as trainers of missionaries to unreached peoples

Training missionaries for ministry among unreached peoples is strategic, as you multiply your own effectiveness by thirty, sixty or even one hundred times (see the Parable of the Sower in Mark 4:3–20). Instead of just you, a lone Christian, going to a particular unreached people group, you are involved in training dozens of others who will go to several unreached people groups.

That's what I'm doing. For the past thirty-five years — first in the United States, then in the Philippines, and now back in the United States — I have been involved in training missionaries for unreached peoples ministries. What a privilege! Instead of reaching only one people group I have the opportunity to help reach literally dozens of people groups vicariously through my students and their ministries. Some of my students are currently reaching Tibetan Buddhists in Katmandu, Nepal; Mongolian peoples in Ulaan Baatar, Mongolia; Muslim groups in Nigeria, Pakistan and Albania; Somali refugees in the United States; various Buddhist and tribal peoples in Myanmar (Burma), Thailand and Cambodia; Chinese university students throughout mainland China; and the Muslim Maranao and Magindanao peoples of the Philippines. And the list goes on.

No wonder I say, "What a privilege!"

Perhaps God is directing you to a similar strategic ministry. I happen to be training missionaries in cross-cultural theology and Bible interpretation, primarily in graduate school (seminary) settings. Your role may be something else entirely. Missionaries who are trainers of frontier missionaries are needed at every level of theological education (from Bible college and below all the way up to graduate seminary), as well as in several other professions. For example, many of the unreached peoples of the world need basic primary health care.

71

If you have a medical background, perhaps God would use you in the training of primary health care workers who could then go to countries and cultures where unreached people groups are located. Another possibility involves the English language. English is highly sought after in many countries where unreached peoples are located. Perhaps you could be involved in training others in Teaching English to Speakers of Other Languages (TESOL).

There are all sorts of possibilities in training others for unreached peoples ministries. But remember two things. First, not everyone can be a trainer. This ministry of training will not be for all who sense the urgency of reaching the unreached. Second, make sure that God is clearly directing you to this type of a ministry. Make sure you are not just trying to avoid the responsibility of what may appear to be a more difficult frontline role in unreached peoples' work. But, if God is clearly directing you to this type of ministry, go for it! There is no question about it — this is a strategic missions ministry. And you don't necessarily have to leave your own country to do it. There may be strategic training centers right in your own area.

Whether or not you stay in your home country as an unreached peoples missionary trainer, you will need to have a missionary sending team behind you.

"Why," some of you are asking, "would a trainer of unreached peoples missionaries in his or her home country need a sending team?" The answer directly relates to the strategic nature of any unreached peoples ministry. If you become a missionary trainer in your home country you may or may not need the financial support of a sending team, but you will *certainly* need their prayer support. Satan does not want those frontier missionaries trained and he will do whatever he can to make your ministry ineffective. The prayers of a support team are essential. I believe that many home-country unreached peoples missionary trainers are not as effective as they might be because they do not have the necessary prayer support.

This need for a sending prayer support team for unreached peoples missionary trainers is especially true if God directs you to a training opportunity outside of your own home country. Developing a missionary sending team is as essential for you as it would be for any missionary desiring to be involved more directly in unreached peoples' ministry. Why? Because leaving your own country brings with it a multitude of problems not encountered in home country ministry. *The closer you are to the "front lines" of unreached peoples ministry, the more prayer support you will need.* Besides, you may need the financial support of the missionary sending team as well!

For those who are sent as apostles to unreached peoples

Let's now address our attention to those of you who are potential "frontline unreached peoples missionaries." Before anything else is said, remember this:

> If God is leading you to be an unreached peoples missionary, then He will also give you *the spiritual gifting for that task.*

Such spiritual gifting will be rooted in the ability to evangelize individuals and plant churches in cross-cultural situations. Such gifting will be grounded in the spiritual gift of apostleship.

"What?" some of you are saying. "Me, an apostle?"

That's right. Maybe even you.

"But wasn't that spiritual gift just for the apostles in the New Testament times?"

No, it wasn't. It's a gift that has been given by God throughout the history of the Church even to the present day. I won't address here all the many details concerning the gift of apostleship. I have written about this subject in another book that you may consult for more detailed information.[1] Rather, let's highlight some of the most important aspects of this spiritual gift that missionaries to unreached peoples need to be especially aware of.

Apostleship: The spiritual gift for missionaries to unreached peoples

What is the spiritual gift of apostleship? Simply stated, this is a spiritual gift given by God to individuals who are involved primarily in cross-cultural evangelism and church planting situations, especially in pioneering, frontline work among unreached peoples. The Apostle Paul lists the gift of apostleship first and foremost among all of the spiritual gifts (see the gift lists in 1 Corinthians 12:28 and Ephesians 4:11). This seems

---

[1] See my *Sent Out! Reclaiming the Spiritual Gift of Apostleship for Missionaries and Churches Today*, 1992. Manila/Pasadena, CA: Church Strengthening Ministry/William Carey Library; available free as a PDF file at: https://drive.google.com/file/d/0B-OE7RzQoZ0kUmFmRThPdHlJUEk/view

to emphasize that churches might not have come into existence in the first place if it had not been for the apostles who had initially gone forth and planted them, especially in cross-cultural situations.

Paul understood his own ministry as an apostle in this way. He himself was involved primarily in cross-cultural missions work to unreached peoples. His own spiritual gift of apostleship compelled him to plant new churches among peoples who had yet to hear the Gospel. As we have already seen in Chapter Two, Paul's heart for unreached peoples gave him his fundamental motivation in life:

> It has always been my ambition to preach the gospel where Christ was not known, so that I would not be building on someone else's foundation (Romans 15:20).

Paul's understanding of apostleship can be seen in his desire to go to Spain, since, "I no longer have any room for work in these regions" (Romans 15:23 *Revised Standard Version*). Paul could have stayed where he was and worked with already reached or reachable peoples. But this is not what an apostle does. F. F. Bruce writes:

> The statement that he "no longer has any room for work in these regions" throws light on Paul's conception of his task. There was certainly much room for further work in the area already evangelized by Paul, but not . . . work of an apostolic nature. The work of an apostle was to

preach the gospel where it had not been heard before and plant churches where none had existed before. When those churches had received sufficient teaching to enable them to understand their Christian status and responsibility, the apostle moved on to continue the same kind of work elsewhere.[2]

Paul's spiritual gift of apostleship compelled him to plant new churches among peoples who had yet to hear the Gospel. Such a ministry was for him, of necessity, cross-cultural. Certainly he has his own apostolic ministry in mind when he places apostles first in his listing of spiritual gifts. Of course, there was more to Paul's gift of apostleship than planting churches cross-culturally. For him the gift also involved teaching canonical doctrine. Because apostles today, unlike Paul, have access to the complete canonical Bible, this aspect of the apostleship gift no longer functions.[3]

Apostle: One sent with authority
It is important to realize that the spiritual gift of apostleship is a gift that comes with special spiritual authority. This authority is rooted in the Old Testament concept of a person who is sent on a task with authority.

The Hebrew word, *shaliach*, from which the New Testament word apostle (Greek: *apostolos*) is derived, referred to someone who functioned as the authorized

---

[2] F. F. Bruce, *Paul: Apostle of the Heart Set Free,* 1977. Grand Rapids, MI: Eerdmans, pp. 314–315.

[3] For more information, see Chapter Four of *Sent Out!*

representative of an individual or a community (in a legal or religious sense), or as the representative of God. Today we think of ambassadors in this way. An ambassador is the authorized representative of a nation. When he is doing his duties he has the full authority to speak on behalf of his nation. It's almost as if he's the President or Prime Minister of his nation, when in fact he is only a government official. This understanding is the same as the Old Testament concept of the *shaliach*, the one sent on a task with authority.

For example, in Isaiah 6:8, when God asks Isaiah, "Whom shall I send? And who will go for us?" God is not requesting someone to be sent on an errand, say, to the store. Rather, God is talking about sending someone on a special task as His authorized representative to the Jewish people. And when Isaiah, hearing God's plea, responds, "Here am I. Send me!" he understands that he is being sent with just such authority. He is God's authorized agent, His *shaliach*.[4]

This, then, is the sense in which the Apostle Paul understands the spiritual gift of apostleship. For Paul, an apostle is one chosen and sent with a special commission as the fully authorized representative of the sender. His own life is a good example of this. Paul, on the road to Damascus, changed from being a *shaliach* of the high priest in Jerusalem to being a *shaliach* of Jesus Christ (see Acts 26:12–18; compare Acts 9:1–19 and 22:21). Paul was the fully authorized representative of the Jewish leadership in Jerusalem sent on a special task to persecute Christians in Damascus. After he met

---

[4] For more information, see Chapter Two of *Sent Out!*

Jesus on the road Paul became the fully authorized representative of Jesus Christ sent on a special task to be a missionary to the unreached Gentiles.

Paul clearly recognized his own authority as an apostle as an authority that came directly from Jesus Christ. This is obvious in the way he began the majority of his letters. For example, in Galatians 1:1 he writes: "Paul, an apostle — sent not from men nor by man, but by Jesus Christ and God the Father." His understanding of his authority as an apostle is also seen in other places in his writings (for example, see 1 Corinthians 9:2 and Galatians 2:8; also 1 Corinthians 15:3–8 and 2 Corinthians 10:8).

The gift of apostleship and you

So what does all of this have to do with those of you who today would be missionaries to the unreached peoples of our world? First of all, it is imperative that you recognize that if God is directing you to frontline unreached peoples work then He will equip you with the spiritual gift you will need. You stand in a long tradition of apostles down through the centuries of church history, who were pioneer missionaries planting churches in cross-cultural situations, primarily among unreached peoples. This is what the Apostle Paul did. This is what you will do. You will have the very same spiritual gift of apostleship that he had. Surprising? It shouldn't be. The task is the same.

As a result, the gift of apostleship is incredibly significant. Why? Because as you work among un-reached people . . .

> ... you have the confidence that you are sent by God on His special mission with *His full backing and authority.*

Isn't that exciting! You will be empowered by God to reach these unreached peoples. You have no cause to feel uncertain about your work, even in the face of overwhelming obstacles. You will do battle against Satan with full confidence. How will you be able to do all this? Because, in your spiritual giftedness, you can claim the very authority of Jesus Christ in your ministry. Why? Because you have been sent forth with His authority (see Matthew 28:18).

Unfortunately, many missionaries today do not see their ministries in terms of "sentness" and authority. All too many are uncertain, unempowered, and lacking confidence. Perhaps this is why the drop-out rate among first-term missionaries approaches fifty percent. But it doesn't have to be this way. If God is directing you to a ministry evangelizing and planting churches among a particular unreached people group, then take hold of the authority that is rightly yours in your gifting as an apostle. Whether or not you actually want to refer to yourself as an apostle is beside the point. The title is not the important thing. The recognition of the gifting, however, is crucial.

How do I know if I have this spiritual gift?

I know what some of you are thinking right now. You are asking something like this: "But how do I know if

I have the gift of apostleship?" This question warrants thorough discussion.

How do you know whether or not you have the spiritual gift of apostle? Of course, in the final analysis, it is the prerogative of God who, through the Holy Spirit, gives spiritual gifts to Christians as He sees fit (1 Corinthians 7:7). But having said that, there are certain factors that should help any Christian answer this important question.

First, are you currently involved in some type of cross-cultural ministry, or do you feel especially directed by God to such a ministry in the future? Do you have a keen interest in people from cultures different than your own? Do you have a particular aptitude for learning languages? Are you currently involved in some kind of ministry with unreached peoples, in international student work, perhaps, or with a newly planted ethnic church in your community? Or, if you are not currently involved in some ministry like this, does the mention of these possibilities truly appeal to you in some significant way? Would you like to be involved in some type of ministry similar to these?

If you answer "yes" to any of these questions, then this may be possible confirmation of the apostleship gift. However, if you are not currently involved in such ministries, nor even remotely interested, then you probably don't have this cross-cultural church planting gift. Why? Because such cross-cultural involvement or interest is a prerequisite for those who would have the gift of apostleship. This involvement, though, may or may not mean working outside your home country. It may involve ministry with an unreached people group in a major urban area within the confines of your native land.

Second, are you currently involved, or truly interested, in cross-cultural evangelism and church planting? Cross-cultural involvement or interest, as mentioned above, does not by itself mean that you have the apostleship gift. Cross-cultural evangelism and church planting are key elements of the gift of apostleship. *Do you have a burning desire to win unreached peoples for the Lord, and plant churches (or fellowship groups) among them where no churches currently exist?* If you have this kind of desire, then it follows that you most likely have this spiritual gift as well.

Now is the time to be honest with yourself. Nothing magical or supernatural happens to a missionary once he or she boards the airplane, boat or bus to go minister among a particular unreached people group. If you are not comfortable being involved in activities that reflect the missionary/apostleship gift prior to your going to an unreached people group, then you probably will not feel comfortable being involved in cross-cultural church planting and evangelism upon your arrival at your destination. In fact, like so many others who struggle in missions, you may be frustrated with your first years of ministry. You may have assumed that the desire to evangelize and plant churches cross-culturally would somehow just happen when you got to the field. Consequently, you will not return for more after your first three or four years of missionary service. A basic maxim concerning the missionary apostleship gift is this:

> If you do not easily exercise the gift, in various ways, *where you are now*, you most likely will not enjoy doing the activities associated with this gift in the future *wherever else you seek to serve*.

Over the years many of my own students, ministering in cross-cultural situations among unreached peoples, have indicated that part of the reason they had been able to "tough it out" during the hard times was because they felt that God had given them a special spiritual gift fit for their oftentimes difficult tasks. It was only later on that they saw this spiritual gift for what it truly was: the gift of apostleship.

May it not be so for you. Know yourself. Know the spiritual gifting that God either has already given you or will give you for the task of reaching unreached peoples.

The Apostle Paul, Mike Boit, and me

God, in His providence, blessed me with the ability to run, and fast. I'm not talking about the sprinting type of fast but rather the middle-distance kind of fast. I'm talking about the mile.

I ran the mile in both high school and college. At that time I was very dedicated to running and this dedication paid off on the track in various victories and high place finishes. While in college my mile times were good enough to qualify me on a few occasions for national collegiate track meets. I was a good runner; not great, but respectable.

I first qualified for a national track meet in my junior year. I was 20 years old. I had won or placed well in lots of races at my alma mater: small Bethel College of St. Paul, Minnesota. This national meet, however, was the "big time." These were the best runners from all over the United States. There were even some current world record holders running in the meet.

As the luck of the draw would have it, a 28-year-old runner from Kenya named Mike Boit was scheduled to run in my race. Boit, at that time, was the current world record-holder in the half-mile and one of the fastest runners in the world at the mile. And I was running against him!

Let me tell you, there is a big difference between the current record holder of Bethel College in Minnesota and the current record holder of the world! Was I frightened? Yes! Did I feel inadequate? You bet I did! Who was I, in the presence of someone like Mike Boit?

Wouldn't you know it, but Mike and I were side by side at the starting line. Usually before a race you shake hands with the runner standing next to you and wish him good luck. But what do you say to a current world record-holder? I was tongue-tied! I shook his hand and mumbled something. Then the starter's gun sounded and the race was on. Was it much of a race? Not really. Everyone knew that Mike Boit would win. I knew it, Mike knew it, and the crowd knew it. But do you know what? No — I didn't win. So what happened? I ran the fastest mile of my life!

I didn't win. I didn't even place in the race. But because of my excitement at being in a race with a world record holder I ran the fastest race of my life. In fact, I set a school record that lasted for over thirty years at what is now called Bethel University. I never ran that fast again.

What does all of this have to do with missions and the Apostle Paul? Everything. When we read about the exploits of the Apostle Paul and the first Christian missionaries, it's easy for us to look upon them as being so great. How can we ever think that we, too, can be missionaries? How can we be apostles? How can we claim to have the same spiritual gift as the Apostle Paul? We look at Paul like I looked at Mike Boit. We feel inadequate. We feel that there is no comparison.

We need to remember, however, that at times Paul had these very same feelings of inadequacy. He felt that he was the least of all the apostles and God's people (see 1 Corinthians 15:9 and, especially, Ephesians 3:8). Yet, Paul was able to do an incredible amount of great missionary work among the unreached peoples of his time.

It's the same for you and me today. Of course we will never be as great as the Apostle Paul. But as did Mike Boit for me, may Paul stimulate each of us to run the fastest race of our lives, so to speak, for the glory of God's Kingdom and for the reaching of many unreached peoples in our world.

Questions to think about

1 Why is the training of missionaries for unreached peoples ministries such an important task? Do you have any spiritual gifts, talents or educational skills that could be used to help train others? What are they?

2 How did the Apostle Paul understand his ministry as an apostle? Why is the spiritual gift of apostleship a gift for missionaries working among unreached peoples today?

3 Do you have the spiritual gift of apostleship? According to this study, what are some of the characteristics of an apostle? How can a missionary today know whether or not he or she has the spiritual gift of apostleship?

4 Why will knowing that their ministries are similar to the Apostle Paul's be helpful and encouraging to missionaries involved today in cross-cultural evangelism and church planting among unreached people groups?

chapter six

WHAT DO YOU DO NOW?

"May [the LORD] give you the desire of your heart
and make all your plans succeed."
PSALM 20:4

WHAT NOW?

The end and the beginning

Here we are, already near the end of this book. Quite a lot has been pressed into this small package. Here's what we've done so far: surveyed the current state of world missions; overviewed missions in the Bible; faced the challenge to make a choice; and examined some guidelines for would-be "senders" and "sent ones." That's a lot! By now your head is probably spinning.

Most of you are undoubtedly wondering, "What do I do now?"

Good question. The answer? You will have to take action. But, before you do anything, take a deep breath and relax. Really! God doesn't expect that all of the world's unreached peoples be reached in the next five minutes, or even in the next five years. He has waited patiently for at least four thousand years. And He isn't expecting that you take the whole weight of the world's unreached peoples upon your shoulders. The missionary task is the responsibility of the entire body of Christ, not yours alone. There's time enough for you to get concrete direction from Him. There's time enough for you to clearly know what He will have you to do, either as a "sender" or as a "sent one." But don't wait too long to find out. The ball is in your court! Eventually you will have to act.

Here then, are some concrete action steps that you can take. These action steps are possibilities for both "senders" and "sent ones." They don't take a lot of time, nor a lot of money. But they are steps that allow you to take action immediately. Don't wait. Why not? Because of this fact:

> Failing to take steps now, when God has touched your heart, may result in missing God's special opportunity for you to become a "sender" or a "sent one."

This is not an idle threat. I'm serious about this and you need to take it seriously as well. Why? Because while you have been reading and studying this book God has been working in your heart in a new way for missions. You are not the same person now as you were when you started reading. Many of you feel the burden right now to be "senders" and "sent ones." There is a real danger if you wait. If you wait and do not follow up your burden with action, then nothing will come of it. The burden you now have will pass and you will go on living your life much as it was before you read this book.

When God prompts you to action, it's imperative that you *do* something.

Do something!

Start a missions prayer-and-support group in your church; adopt an unreached people group; go on a short-term missions trip; read some more books on missions. We'll talk about all of these possibilities in this chapter. Most of these activities involve minimum cost and effort. The main thing now is for you to put your burden for unreached peoples into action. It will be a new beginning for you.

Start a missions prayer-and-support group
The best way to keep your own missions interest alive is to get together with other like-minded people. You probably already have some Christian friends who are also interested in missions. Spend time with them. Share with each other your common interest in missions. You could have everybody read this book so that you all begin on common ground. Study the Bible yourselves and examine in more detail what God's heart really is. Begin praying together for specific countries, unreached people groups and missionaries. Begin giving money to missionaries and missions projects that minister to unreached peoples.

We already talked about a senders' group in Chapter Four. A missions prayer-and-support group may soon grow into a senders' group, zeroing in on specific missionaries and specific unreached people groups. For those of you who would be "sent ones" there is no better way to raise up a personal support team of senders than to begin a missions prayer-and-support group.

Do you have the burden to get your church more interested in missions? Again, starting a missions prayer-and-support group within your church is a great way to motivate your entire church for missions. It's about the best way that I know of to get a church excited about missions. As the missions prayer-and-support group grows, soon more and more church members will want to get involved with missions.

I have seen this happen many times in the lives of my students. One of my students will come up to me and say that he is interested in missions but his church is not. Here's a typical conversation:

Student: "Dr. Caldwell, what should I do? Should I find a more missions-minded church?"

Caldwell: "No — don't leave your church. Instead, start a missions prayer-and-support group with your friends in the church."

Student: "But nobody else is interested in missions."

Caldwell: "Nevertheless, see if you can start a missions prayer-and-support group. There will always be at least a handful of interested members. You just have to find them."

Student: "Well, I'll try."

A few months pass and he comes back and tells me that not only does he have a great missions support group going, but that the entire church is starting to get excited about missions. In fact, they want to send their own missionary and he is the first candidate! Really, this story has happened over and over again. Do you feel discouraged about a lack of missions interest in your church? Begin a missions prayer-and-support group and you can help change all of that.

In addition, there are lots of resources to help guide your missions prayer-and-support group. Check out the websites of the Joshua Project (www.joshuaproject.net), Operation World (www.operationworld.org), and the Global Prayer Digest (www.globalprayerdigest.org) for some good prayer information.

Adopt an unreached people group

People often adopt children and raise them as their own. Using that same analogy, groups of Christians can "adopt" a specific unreached people group and care for them in special ways: making a commitment to pray; giving financially; and, where possible, sending personnel to see them reached. It's really very easy to adopt an unreached people group. God may have already given you a burden for a particular group isolated by geography or culture. If that is the case, then what you need to do now is learn all you can about that group and intelligently pray for them. You will also want your missions prayer-and-support team to adopt this group as their own as well. Your church too may want to adopt this group. As you learn more and pray more about your unreached people group, God will deepen your burden for them. Then perhaps you, or one from your prayer group or church, will want to actually go and take the Good News to this unreached people group. Unbelievable? No, it's happened many times. Or, you may want to find out about others who are planning to go to this group — or who are already there — so that you can pray for these missionaries, and perhaps even offer them financial assistance. Someday you yourself may want to visit the country and the very region where your adopted group is located, to learn first-hand about the group. The possibilities are endless, and exciting!

Go on a short-term missions trip
If you have not already done so, you will want to get some exposure to another culture. Why? Because this exposure will make you more sensitive to peoples of other cultures and, more importantly, it will help you pray more intelligently for missions. Both "senders" and potential "sent ones" can greatly benefit from a short-term missions trip. The "senders" will gain insights that will help them relate better to the experiences and situations faced by missionaries they will be supporting. And in the midst of this cross-cultural exposure the potential "sent ones" may receive special confirmation concerning whether or not cross-cultural living is God's desire for them.

A short-term missions trip doesn't have to be fancy or expensive. In the United States, most Christians have easy access to short-term missions trip opportunities. In many parts of the world, like the Philippines, there are missions agencies and churches that can assist you in finding an opening for missions exposure. The situation is not necessarily the same for Christians elsewhere in the world. Nevertheless, Christians in most countries can gain exposure to other peoples and cultures either in their own country, or in an adjacent country, without too much expense. Be creative! Invite your entire missions prayer-and-support team. Invite the young people from your church. Be prepared for changed lives.

Read a book

Where do you go from here? One of the best places is to a library or bookstore. There are lots of good books on missions, books that can help you better understand what you need to do as either a "sender" or as a "sent one." In the next few pages I have highlighted — and given short summaries — of some that I consider to be among the most important missions books. Read them! If you read them all you will know just about everything there is to be learned from books about missions. They will be of immense help to you as you attempt to answer the question, "What do I do now?" Most of these books may be available through your local Christian bookstore or through the Internet at either www.amazon.com or www.missionbooks.org.

In alphabetical order, by title, the books are as follows:

Let the Nations be Glad! The Supremacy of God in Missions
3rd edition by John Piper, Baker Book House, 2010.
This book pleads for the church to catch a God-centered vision for engaging in world evangelization. *Let the Nations be Glad!* has provided — for thousands of Bible college and seminary students, missionaries, and pastors — a sound theological foundation concerning missions and the Church, with the watchword, "Missions exist

because worship doesn't." Drawing on texts from the Old and New Testaments, Piper demonstrates that worship is the ultimate goal of the church and that proper worship drives missionary outreach. Essential reading for all those involved in or preparing for missions work, whether they are "senders" or "sent ones."

Perspectives on the World Christian Movement: A Reader
4th revised edition edited by Ralph D. Winter and
Steven C. Hawthorne, William Carey Library, 2009.

Used in over a hundred schools and many special courses, this text was designed to be the missionary platform of essential knowledge for all serious Christians who have had only a secular education. It is a library of information for the biblical, historical, cultural, and strategic aspects of missions in today's world. It contains a hundred and seventy articles written by a hundred and fifty different authors, and is one of the basic books any Christian seriously interested in missions should read. "Sent ones" should become familiar with much of the material in this book; motivated "senders" will also immensely benefit from it, though it is sometimes academic and technical.

Pray for the World
by Molly Wall, InterVarsity Press, 2015.

Prayer changes things! Abridged from the 7th edition of *Operation World*, this book is a unique resource for Christians who want God to use their prayers to change the world. A prayer directory covering every country in the world combines with a survey of prayer burdens both for the church and for those it needs to reach in each country. Background facts and figures about populations, peoples, economies, politics, religions and churches, are backed up by detailed maps and graphs. Read and rejoice over all that God has already done among the nations, but also pray and become a part of what yet needs to be done before the Gospel is effectively proclaimed to the ends of the earth. Senders, this one's especially for you! It's a great book for your own prayer times as well as for use by your missions prayer-and-support group.

Radical. Taking Back Your Faith from the American Dream
by David Platt, Multnomah Books, 2010.

This book was written primarily for an American audience but it is really for every Christian who is serious about reaching the unreached peoples today. Platt challenges all Christians to consider with an open heart how we have manipulated the gospel to fit our own cultural preferences. He reminds us how the early church abandoned everything for the sake of the gospel and how we can return to what it truly means to be a disciple of Jesus in today's world.

SENT OUT! Reclaiming the Spiritual Gift of Apostleship for Missionaries and Churches Today
by Larry W. Caldwell, William Carey Library, 1992.
Available free as a PDF file at: https://drive.google.com/file/ d/0B-OE7RzQoZ0kUmFmRThPdHlJUEk/view

Most evangelicals today do not know what to do with the spiritual gift of apostleship. While they know that this gift somehow functioned in the Early Church of the New Testament, they are very confused about how it functions, or should function, in the Church today.

Many have gone so far as to say that the gift is no longer valid for today, that it somehow ceased after the closing of the New Testament canon. In *Sent Out*! I attempt to shed new light on this confusion and analyze the biblical evidence from the perspectives of both theology and missiology. My conclusion is that apostleship is a legitimate spiritual gift for the mission of the church today. Beneficial reading for both "senders" and "sent ones," though it is academic and technical.

Serving as Senders—Today: Six Ways to Support Your Missionaries

by Neal Pirolo, Emmaus Road, 2012.

This key book makes the strategic point that "senders" are as important to the cause of missions as the frontline missionaries. It is a book crammed with solid, exciting insights on the most hurting link in today's mission movement. Pirolo gives insights into six areas of missionary support: moral, logistical, financial, prayer, communication, and re-entry. Senders, you must read this book!

Surf the Internet

Where do you go from here? Another great source is the Internet. While there is lots of information about missions found on the Internet, I have listed here three of the most pertinent websites for unreached peoples information and strategy, along with a short summary of what can be found on that website. Take some time to carefully explore these sites. Together they are a goldmine of information about unreached people groups and how to reach them.

Joshua Project

(www.joshuaproject.net)

Joshua Project is the most comprehensive website available for specific unreached peoples research. This is the place for any "sender" or "sent one" to start. Joshua Project is a research initiative seeking to highlight the ethnic people groups of the world with the least followers of Christ. Accurate, regularly updated ethnic people group information is critical for understanding and completing the Great Commission.

Joshua Project seeks to answer the questions that result from the Great Commission's call to make disciples among every nation or people group: 1) Who are the ethnic people groups of the world? 2) Which people groups still need an initial church-planting movement in their midst? And 3) What ministry resources are available to help outreach among the least-reached? Joshua Project gathers, integrates and shares people group information to encourage pioneer church-planting movements among every ethnic group and to facilitate effective coordination of mission agency efforts. Joshua Project compiles the work of numerous missions researchers to develop a list of all ethnic peoples that is as complete as possible.

The Traveling Team — Missions Resource Library

(www.thetravelingteam.org/resources)

The Traveling Team's primary purpose is to mobilize university students for unreached peoples ministry. Their "Missions Resource Library" is jam-packed full of topics and resources that are indispensible for any individual Christian or church who is interested in gaining more knowledge about missions. Topics include: "Biblical Foundation," "History of Missions," "Obstacles to Mission," "Missional Living," and "State of the World." Be prepared to spend a lot of time on this website as you gain lots of new and helpful information about missions.

International Journal of Frontier Missions — Archives

(www.ijfm.org/archives.htm)

The *International Journal of Frontier Missions* (IJFM) is the "go to" source for all the latest in-depth and more scholarly writing on unreached peoples. The archives of the IJFM holds almost forty years of perceptive articles about who the unreached peoples are and, more importantly, how to reach them. Better yet, all of the articles are free and downloadable as PDF files. Spend time perusing some of the articles. You won't be disappointed. The IJFM is the official journal of the International Society for Frontier Missiology.

Take a course

Still wanting to do more? For those of you really wanting to "do something," I highly recommmend taking either the "Perspectives" or the "Kairos" course, depending on where you live. Both courses are available worldwide and in a number of different languages. Contact their websites at www.perspectives.org or www.simplymobilizing.com for more information. You will be glad you did!

Conclusion

There are indeed lots of action steps that you can take. The suggestions listed in the previous pages could be just the first steps towards the next exciting chapter of your life for the Lord. Again, it's up to you. You're the one who must respond. I can't do it for you. No other person can do it for you. You must do it yourself.

God has given us the tremendous privilege of having a part in the great task of reaching the remaining 7,000 unreached people groups of our world. God has given us a marvelous opportunity to partake, in our own small ways, in the eternal destiny of two billion individuals. What a privilege indeed! Go for it!

INSIGHT:

Short-term trips and spiritual gifts

A short-term missions trip can be a wonderful learning experience, not only about missions, but about your own spiritual gifting as well. Let me give two examples from my own life.

Before my last year in seminary my wife and I traveled to the Philippines, for one year, to teach at a small Bible college. Both my wife and I felt God leading us to missionary work. God had also been slowly revealing to me that some of my spiritual gifting lay in the area of teaching. This short-term year was a great time for us. It confirmed in me that teaching was indeed my gifting and also that we as a couple should become involved in long-term cross-cultural missions work. It also helped us discover some of our weaknesses, areas that we needed to work on and grow in.

Two years later, when my wife and I spent a year teaching English in the People's Republic of China, it was again a time for me to test my spiritual gifts. In the Philippines my teaching gift had been confirmed. Now, in China, I was attempting to discover if I had some of the gifts necessary for frontline unreached peoples ministry. Well, to make a long story short, I discovered that I did not. I led no Chinese to the Lord. I planted no churches. In fact, I discovered that it wasn't even very easy for me to talk about Christianity with many of my Chinese students. But, once again, my teaching gift was confirmed. I realized then that frontline unreached peoples ministry wasn't my particular gifting, but that my zeal for unreached peoples could be channeled into teaching those who would be on the frontlines.

A short-term missions experience may be helpful to you, as well. The experience may help you discover your spiritual gifting and the level of cross-cultural involvement that God desires for you.

Short-term missions trips — check them out!

Questions to think about

1   Make a list of five Christian friends who could join you as the core members of a missions prayer-and-support group. How will you go about recruiting these potential members? When and where will your first meeting be held? For whom will you pray?

2   Do you feel a burden for, or have an interest in, a particular unreached people group? Is God leading you to adopt this people group as your own special interest group, for whom you can pray, and about whom you can do some research? How can you get your missions prayer-and-support group and church to adopt this group as well?

3   Are any short-term opportunities for ministry open to you? What are they? What will you have to do to take advantage of them?

4   What is the next book that you plan to read on missions? How will you get it and when will you start reading it? When will you look up the listed websites on your computer?

About the Author

Larry, and his wife Mary, lived in Asia off and on for 30 years, with over 20 years in Manila, Philippines, as missionaries with Converge Worldwide (formerly Baptist General Conference). In Manila he was Professor of Missions and Bible Interpretation at the Asian Theological Seminary; he also served as Academic Dean for five years. In addition, Larry edited the Journal of Asian Mission as well as directed the Doctor of Missiology (D.Miss.) Program of the Asia Graduate School of Theology.

In June of 2011, Larry and Mary returned to the USA where Larry became the Director of Training and Strategy for Converge Worldwide, as well as (in 2015) Chief Academic Officer and Dean, and Professor of Intercultural Studies and Bible Interpretation, at Sioux Falls Seminary, located in Sioux Falls, South Dakota. Larry continues to teach regularly on contextualization and cross-cultural Bible interpretation at seminaries and training institutions around the world.

Larry has published several books as well as dozens of articles found in many Western and Asian journals, as well as presented academic papers at missiological and theological meetings both in Asia and in the United States. One of his most recent books, *Doing Bible Interpretation! Making the Bible Come Alive for Yourself and Your People* (2016) is available on Amazon.com in both English and Spanish. Some of his writings, especially on the topic of ethnohermeneutics, can be freely downloaded from https://sfseminary.edu/about-the-seminary/faculty-and-staff/larry-caldwell/

Larry is an avid runner. He also enjoys biking, cross-country skiing, golfing and snowshoeing. Larry and Mary have four adult children and two grandchildren.

Notes

Notes

We would love to hear from you!

Please share with us how this book
has helped or blessed you.

You can send us your comments and suggestions
through any of the following channels:

Landline: +63(2) 8531-4303 loc. 304
Mobile: +63918 298-4819
Email: inquire@omflit.com
Website: www.omflit.com

You may also join our online conversations:

omflit

Subscribe to our e-newsletter by sending an email to:
newchapters@omflit.com

You may order more books through these channels:
Mobile: +63915 919-1262
Email: estore@omflit.com
Online store: www.omflit.com

OMF LITERATURE INC.
Publishing Truth.
Shaping Generations.
www.OMFLit.com

Made in the USA
Monee, IL
15 January 2022

88864701R00066